Health
Grade Five

W9-BEJ-092

Table of Contents

The school curriculum designates the topics taught to students, with the most stress placed on the core subjects of language arts and math. Health is the subject usually taught in the spare days between units in order to meet standards. However, health teaches students valuable life skills that they need to learn to develop healthy living habits. These skills will help students make responsible choices that affect their daily lives.

In this series, *Health,* information was compiled to supplement the required standards for health in each grade level. The activities were selected to complement the core subjects. So, instead of fitting health into the curriculum in one or two specific units, it can be introduced in any subject throughout the year. (The Curriculum Correlation chart on page 2 will help you determine which activities to incorporate into your core subjects.) The activities are fun and challenging, thereby avoiding the stigma of "boring" health worksheets. Many activities are open-ended so that students will have to think about, evaluate, and apply healthy habits to their daily lives. Moreover, introducing the activities into the core classes may reinforce positive habits.

This book focuses on the ten body systems. Unit 1 provides information on the nervous and integumentary systems. Most of the information deals with the five senses. Unit 2 explores the skeletal and muscular systems. Here, students learn about such topics as the functions of the bones and muscles, as well as the importance of exercising. Unit 3 introduces the remaining six body systems: circulatory, digestive, excretory, respiratory, endocrine, and reproductive. As students learn about the functions of their bodies throughout the year, it will encourage safe and healthy habits. They will more likely remember the information, and thereby, apply it to their daily lives— the goal of any health program.

Health 5, SV 2707-3

Health
Grade Five
Curriculum Correlation

Activity	Math	Language Arts	Social Studies	Science	Physical Education
Unit 1: Your Body Makes Sense					
Levels of Organization	classifying			animals plants	
Cells in Your Body		use pictures	research tools		
The Body Systems	use charts		research tools		
Your Sense of Smell		comprehension		matter	
Odor Test	measurement			matter	
Your Sense of Sight		use pictures comprehension		light	
Your Sense of Touch		comprehension			
The Integumentary System	use charts	comprehension		experiment	
Your Sense of Hearing		sequence use pictures		sound	
Hear, Hear!		composition	music	sound	
Decibels	number sense	use pictures			
Your Sense of Taste	use charts	sequence use pictures			
Taste and Smell	collect data	comprehension	cultures	matter	
Sense Organs and the Brain	measurement use charts			experiment	
Sensory Match		vocabulary			
Unit 2: Systems That Shape You					
The Skeletal System		vocabulary			exercise
How Bones Join		use pictures comprehension			exercise
Skeleton Skills		use pictures	research tools		
The Muscular System		vocabulary comprehension			exercise
Kinds of Muscles		use pictures	research tools		exercise
Warm Up and Cool Down	use charts				exercise
Exercise and Muscles	measurement	comprehension			exercise
Muscle Tone	measurement use charts	comprehension		experiment	exercise
Unit 3: All Systems Go!					
The Circulatory System		comprehension			
The Flow of Blood		use pictures sequence	research tools		
Blood Cells	number sense measurement	comprehension		space	
The Digestive System		use pictures sequence	research tools	matter	
Saliva	use charts	comprehension		matter experiment	
The Excretory System	measurement	sequence		matter experiment	
The Respiratory System		vocabulary		matter	
Respiration Rates	use charts measurement			experiment	exercise
Are You a Windbag?	measurement			experiment	
The Endocrine System	use graphs measurement		family		
The Reproductive System	use charts percentage		family		
Systems Working Together		vocabulary		matter	
What Keeps You Healthy?		vocabulary			exercise

Name _____   Date _____

Health Assessment

• •

✎**Darken the circle beside the answer that correctly completes each statement.**

1. A _____ is the first of five levels of organization in living things.
- Ⓐ organ
- Ⓑ tissue
- Ⓒ system
- Ⓓ cell

2. A group of organs working together make up a _____.
- Ⓐ body system
- Ⓑ circulation chart
- Ⓒ cell guide
- Ⓓ muscle group

3. The _____ is the body part that identifies the messages of all the senses.
- Ⓐ heart
- Ⓑ brain
- Ⓒ hands
- Ⓓ spinal column

4. The sense of touch tells about how things feel, temperature, pressure, and _____.
- Ⓐ pain
- Ⓑ color
- Ⓒ smell
- Ⓓ noise

5. The _____ helps keep disease from entering the body.
- Ⓐ heat
- Ⓑ lungs
- Ⓒ skin
- Ⓓ hair

6. Sound is measured in units called _____.
- Ⓐ meters
- Ⓑ quarts
- Ⓒ receptors
- Ⓓ decibels

7. The tongue can taste bitter, sweet, salty, and _____ flavors.
- Ⓐ pepper
- Ⓑ pickle
- Ⓒ sour
- Ⓓ chocolate

Go on to the next page.

Health Assessment, p. 2

8. The skeleton _____ the body.
ⓐ forms
ⓑ supports
ⓒ protects
ⓓ all of the above

9. The _____ system moves materials to all parts of your body.
ⓐ integumentary
ⓑ circulatory
ⓒ nervous
ⓓ muscular

10. The excretory system removes _____ from the body.
ⓐ blood
ⓑ heat
ⓒ waste
ⓓ saliva

11. When you breathe in, your body takes in _____.
ⓐ oxygen
ⓑ carbon dioxide
ⓒ salt
ⓓ wastes

12. The endocrine system controls the _____ of the body.
ⓐ movement
ⓑ growth
ⓒ diseases
ⓓ senses

13. _____ is the passing of characteristics and traits from parents to children.
ⓐ Respiration
ⓑ Heredity
ⓒ Vibration
ⓓ Tissue

14. All of your health habits are called a _____.
ⓐ movement
ⓑ meeting
ⓒ system
ⓓ lifestyle

4

Name _____ Date _____

Levels of Organization

All living things have five different levels of organization. The *cell* is the first of five levels of organization. Groups of cells that have the same structure and do the same job are called *tissues*. The muscle in your biceps—in the front of your arm— is an example of a tissue. An *organ* is a group of different kinds of tissues working together to do a specific job. Your heart is an example of an organ. A *system* is a group of organs working together to do a job. Your respiratory system, for example, is responsible for your breathing. Your entire body is an example of the highest level of organization—the *organism*.

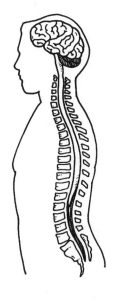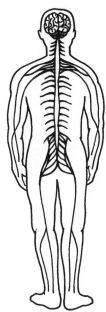

✎Classify each thing listed below by using one of these terms: *cell, tissue, organ, system, organism.*

1. stomach _____ **2.** muscle _____

3. blood _____ **4.** lung _____

5. leaf _____ **6.** oak tree _____

7. digestive _____ **8.** nervous _____

9. nerve _____ **10.** tibia _____

11. tree bark _____ **12.** amoeba _____

Name _____ Date _____

Cells in Your Body

✎Your body has many kinds of cells that do different jobs. Under each picture, write the correct name using the words in the box. You may use a resource book to look up cells that you do not recognize.

1.

_____

2.

_____

3.

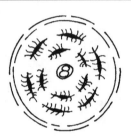

_____

4.

_____

5.

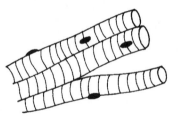

_____

6.

_____

7.

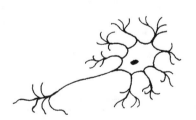

_____

8.

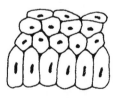

_____

skeletal muscle cells	heart muscle cells	covering cells
white blood cells	red blood cells	neurons
bone cells	smooth muscle cells	

The Body Systems

··

A body system is a group of organs that work together to do a job. For example, the stomach and intestines are parts of the digestive system that help break down the food that you eat. Your body has ten systems. They are the skeletal system, muscular system, digestive system, nervous system, excretory system, respiratory system, circulatory system, endocrine system, reproductive system, and integumentary system.

✎**Use a science book or encyclopedia to label each system in the chart.**

System	Function
1.	This system transports materials to all parts of the body.
2.	Without this system, you couldn't move from place to place or lift things.
3.	This system regulates growth and development and helps control some body functions.
4.	Bones of this system give your body its shape and provide support. They also protect internal organs.
5.	The skin, hair, and nails of this system provide a protective layer for your body.
6.	This system provides a way for adults to produce offspring.
7.	This system takes in oxygen and releases carbon dioxide.
8.	The food you eat must be broken down by this system into nutrients your body cells can use.
9.	This system removes the wastes produced by your body cells.
10.	This system controls your body and helps you respond to your environment.

Your Sense of Smell

The human body collects information using the five senses—sight, smell, hearing, taste, and touch. The nervous system is the system that helps our body respond to the environment. The brain is the main organ of the nervous system. The different body organs send messages through the nerves to the brain. The brain sorts out the messages to tell the body how to react.

The nose is the sense organ for the sense of smell. There are many nerve cells in the nose that take the information about odors to the olfactory nerve. It is the main nerve for the sense of smell. The olfactory nerve carries the information to the brain. The brain will then give out information about what the smell is. It can sense 50 different smells.

✎Answer these questions.

1. What are the five senses?

_____

_____

2. What is the main organ of the nervous system?

_____

_____

3. How do you think a cold affects the sensory nerve cells in your nose?

_____

_____

Name _____ Date _____

Odor Test

To find out how quickly you smell something, try this activity.

Materials:

pencil
record sheet
clock with second hand
saucer
perfume

Do This:

1. Your teacher will divide the class into two groups. Half the class will participate in the experiment while the other half records the data. Then, you will switch roles and repeat the activity.

2. As a participant, you will shut your eyes. Your teacher will then pour some perfume into a saucer.

3. Raise your hand when you first smell the perfume. Keep your hand raised until a hand count has been taken.

4. As a recorder, count and record the number of people who have their hands raised at each 15-second interval. Then enter your data on the chart.

5. Graph the data from your chart.

Seconds	Number of People
15	
30	
45	
60	
75	
90	
105	
120	
135	
150	
165	
180	

Go on to the next page.

Unit 1: Your Body Makes Sense
Health 5, SV 2707-3

Odor Test, p. 2

✎**Answer these questions.**

A. 1. How long did it take the first participant to notice the perfume odor?

_____

2. How long was it before everyone noticed the odor?

_____

3. Why do you think the participants took different amounts of time to detect the odor?

_____

_____

_____

_____

_____

B. **Do the experiment once more with the perfume at the opposite side of the room. Have all the students keep the same seat that they had for the first experiment. Do the results of your second experiment support your conclusion? Explain.**

_____

_____

_____

_____

Name _____ Date _____

Your Sense of Sight

....

    Your eyes are the sense organs that help you see. They send messages of pictures you see to the brain. Many tissues work together to make up the eye.

    The iris is the colored part of your eye. The pupil is the opening in the iris. It controls the amount of light that enters the eye. It grows bigger to help you see in dim light. The pupil grows smaller to keep too much light from harming the eye. The lens is inside the eye. It focuses the light on the retina, the sensory nerves on the back of the eyeball. The retina collects all the pictures and sends them to the optic nerve. The optic nerve then sends the pictures to the brain. The brain then decodes the pictures to tell us what we see.

✎**Label the parts of the eye.**

1. _____

2. _____

3. _____

4. _____

5. _____

Your Sense of Touch

••

The sense of touch tells us when our body has made contact with another object. The sense of touch can give us information about the things we touch, and it tells us about temperature, pain, and pressure.

The skin is the largest sense organ. Within the skin are nerve endings that give us information about touch. There are more nerves in some parts of the body than in others. The fingers have more nerves for touch than other parts of the skin. Also, some nerves are deep inside the skin, while others are on the surface. If you touch your skin lightly, you feel touch. If you push harder on your skin, you will stimulate the nerves deeper in the skin. You will feel pressure and then pain.

The information of touch is carried by the nerve cells to the spinal cord. Then the message is moved to the brain. The brain sends signals to the body that tell it what to do. For example, suppose you touch a hot pan. Sensory nerves send the information of heat to the spinal cord. The spinal cord sends the message to the brain. The brain tells the muscles in your arm to move away from the heat. If you could not feel the heat or the pain, you would get hurt very easily.

✎Answer these questions.

1. What four things do the nerve endings in the skin react to?

_____

_____

2. Why do you think there are more nerve ending in the fingers than in other parts of the skin?

_____

_____

3. What would happen to someone touching a hot pan if that person did not have a sense of touch?

_____

_____

Name _____ Date _____

The Integumentary System

The integumentary system is the group of tissues and organs that protect the body. The skin, hair, and nails are part of this system. Using an apple, find out how the skin protects the body from disease.

Materials:

two small paper plates
crayon or marking pen
two fresh apples
one rotten apple
plastic knife

Do This:

1. Label one of the paper plates *uncut skin.* Label the other one *cut skin.*
2. Place a fresh apple on each paper plate.
3. Cut a badly spoiled piece off the rotten apple.
4. Cut a small piece of the skin off the apple labeled *cut skin.* Rub the piece of rotten apple on the area where the skin has been removed. Some of the rotten apple should stick to the fresh apple.
5. Next, rub the same piece of the rotten apple on the apple labeled *uncut skin.*
6. Throw away the small pieces of the apple and the rest of the rotten apple. Clean up your area and wash your hands.
7. Put the paper plates with the apples aside. Observe the cut and uncut apples each day for one week. Record your observations in the table on the next page.

Go on to the next page.

Name _____ Date _____

The Integumentary System, p. 2

Observations		
Day	**Apple with Cut Skin**	**Apple with Uncut Skin**
1		
2		
3		
4		
5		
6		
7		

✎**Answer these questions.**

1. Describe what happened to the cut and uncut apples. How can you explain a difference in the two apples?

_____

_____

_____

_____

2. How is your skin like the skin of an apple?

_____

_____

_____

_____

Name _____ Date _____

Your Sense of Hearing

✎The pictures show how you hear a dog when it barks. The sentences tell about the pictures. The sentences are not in the correct order. Write numbers to show the correct order of the sentences.

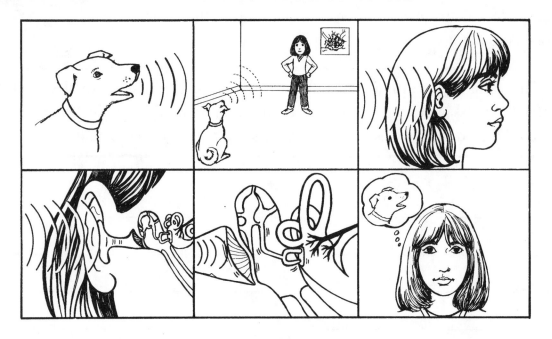

_____ The vibrating vocal cords bump the air molecules. These molecules start to vibrate. Sound waves form. They travel from the dog.

_____ The sound waves push against the eardrum and make it vibrate. The vibrating eardrum passes along the vibrations to three tiny bones, a liquid, and thousands of nerve endings.

_____ The dog barks. Its breath passes out of its throat and makes its vocal cords vibrate.

_____ The outer ear collects the sound waves. It brings them into the narrow canal inside the ear.

_____ Messages about the vibrations are sent along a large nerve to your brain. You recognize the sound as barking.

_____ Sound waves from the dog's vocal cords reach your ears.

Name _____ Date _____

Hear, Hear!

•••

✎**Complete these exercises.**

A.   Pamela is listening to an orchestra. For her to hear the music, many things happen in her body. Below is a scrambled list of some of these events. Rewrite the events in order from the first thing that happens to the last.

> The vibrating eardrum passes the message to nearby bones. Auditory nerves carry the message to the brain. Sound vibrations caused by the instruments reach the eardrum. Bones vibrate and pass the message to the auditory nerve.

_____

_____

_____

_____

B.   Do you have a favorite sound? If you don't have one, choose a sound that you dislike.

1. Write a two-line poem that describes this sound.
Here is an example:

One of my favorite things
Is to hear the sweet song that my parakeet sings.

_____

_____

2. If you cup your hands behind your ears when you listen to the sound you described, do you think the sound would be louder or softer? _____

Explain your answer. _____

_____

_____

Decibels

• •

Roaring, humming, honking, giggling—sounds are all around us. Sounds can be pleasing, like a cat purring when you stroke it. And sounds can be annoying, like a phone ringing and ringing. But sounds can also be damaging. Noise can make your head hurt and make you feel bad all over. Very loud sounds can damage your ears and can even make you lose your hearing.

Sound is measured in units called *decibels*. Decibels begin at 0 for sounds that a human with normal hearing would not be able to hear. Something very quiet, such as whispering, is about 10 decibels. As sounds get louder, the number of decibels gets higher. At a certain point, sounds become so loud that they are felt as pain rather than heard as sounds. The chart shows some common sound levels.

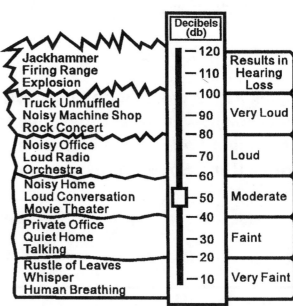

✎ Answer these questions.

1. Sounds that are 100 decibels or higher can cause hearing loss. What sounds might damage hearing?

   _____

   _____

   _____

2. How much louder than whispering is talking?

   _____

   _____

3. How many decibels do you think a shout would be?

   _____

Your Sense of Taste

There are many sensory nerves in your mouth. They are all on the tongue. The ends of the cells are called *taste buds.* They help sense flavors that are salty, sweet, sour, or bitter. The nerves send the message to the brain, and the brain tells what flavors are in your mouth.

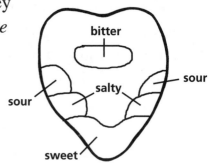

✎**Look at the words in the box. Write them in the chart under *Taste Order* to show in what order they taste food. Then write the letters in the column *Code Words* in the blanks. Leave a blank space between the words. (Hint: Some words may have more blanks than you need.)**

Word Box

brain   taste buds   taste nerves

Taste Order	Code Words											
1.	__	__	__	__	__	__	__	__	__	__	__	__
	1	2	3	4	5	6	7	8	9	10	11	12
2.	__	__	__	__	__	__	__	__	__	__	__	__
	13	14	15	16	17	18	19	20	21	22	23	24
3.	__	__	__	__	__	__	__	__	__	__	__	__
	25	26	27	28	29	30	31	32	33	34	35	36

4. A secret code word contains these coded letters: 28, 5, 25, 4, 13, 21. Unscramble them for the secret word: _____.

Name _____ Date _____

Taste and Smell

Materials:

blindfold   six toothpicks

two paper cups of water   two each of three food samples

(You may wish to use six different foods and keep the cups covered

so that the tasters do not see the foods before they taste them.)

Do This:

1. Your teacher will give you and your partner three food samples, each in a numbered cup.

2. Decide who will be the taster and who will be the recorder. The taster should be blindfolded.

3. Using a toothpick, pick up a small amount of one food sample. Tell the taster to hold his or her nose. Then, place the food on the taster's tongue.

4. Tell the taster to roll the sample on his or her tongue. Then, ask the taster to identify the type of taste and to name the food. Record the response in your chart.

5. Repeat steps 3 and 4 with each food sample. Have the taster drink some water after each sample to clear the taste buds. Use a new toothpick each time.

6. Switch places with the taster, and repeat the activity.

	Food Sample	**Food Identified**
1.	_____	_____
2.	_____	_____
3.	_____	_____

	Food Sample	**Food Identified**
1.	_____	_____
2.	_____	_____
3.	_____	_____

Go on to the next page.

Taste and Smell, p. 2

✎**Answer these questions.**

1. Were there any food samples that the tasters could not identify?

_____

_____

_____

2. Which ones did each taster guess correctly?

_____

_____

_____

3. Why might a taster have difficulty identifying some of the foods?

_____

_____

_____

4. Would the results be the same if the tasters could see the food? Why or why not?

_____

_____

_____

5. Would the results be the same if the tasters did not hold their noses?
Why or why not?

_____

_____

_____

Name _____ Date _____

Sense Organs and the Brain

Your nervous system controls your reactions. In this activity, you and a partner will measure the time it takes for a person to react.

Materials:

meter stick   nontransparent tape, such as masking tape

Do This:

1. Wrap the tape around the stick so that one piece is lined up with the 30 cm mark and the other with the 40 cm mark.

2. One partner should sit with his or her writing arm resting on a desk. The arm should extend beyond the edge of the desk to a point midway between the wrist and elbow.

3. The other partner should stand holding the meter stick at the 100 cm mark. The meter stick should hang within grasp of the seated partner at the 30 cm mark.

4. The seated partner should concentrate on the 40 cm tape mark and be ready to snap his or her fingers shut on that mark when the meter stick starts falling.

5. The standing partner should release the stick without warning. The seated partner should grab the stick. Measure how far the stick fell from the 30 cm mark.

6. Switch places and repeat the above steps.

7. What you measured was the reaction distance. To find the reaction time, use the table shown.

8. Record your results on the chart below.

DISTANCE OF FALL (cm)	TIME OF FALL (s)
1	0.045
2	0.064
3	0.078
4	0.090
5	0.101
6	0.110
7	0.120
8	0.128
9	0.136
10	0.143
11	0.150
12	0.157
13	0.163
14	0.169
15	0.175
16	0.181
17	0.186
18	0.192
19	0.197
20	0.202
21	0.207
22	0.212
23	0.217
24	0.221
25	0.226
26	0.230
27	0.235
28	0.239
29	0.243
30	0.247
31	0.252
32	0.256
33	0.259
34	0.263
35	0.267
36	0.271
37	0.275
38	0.279
39	0.282
40	0.286

	Distance	Time
You		
Partner		

✎Answer these questions.

1. Who had the faster reaction time?

_____

2. How did your senses and muscles work together in this activity?

_____

Name _____ Date _____

Sensory Match

✎**On the blank line next to each word or phrase on the left, write the letter of its matching phrase from the column on the right.**

1. vibrate _____

2. taste buds _____

3. lens _____

4. cells _____

5. auditory nerve _____

6. pupil _____

7. iris _____

8. spinal cord _____

9. optic nerve _____

10. nervous system _____

11. nucleus _____

12. tissue _____

13. organ _____

14. outer ear _____

15. body system _____

a. the nerve that carries sound messages to the brain

b. groups of organs that work together

c. the sense organs, nerves, brain, and spinal cord

d. a large nerve that carries messages to the brain

e. the opening in the center of the iris

f. group of tissues that works together

g. the part of a cell that controls its activities

h. groups of cells on the tongue

i. the part of the eye that changes light into a pattern

j. the nerve that carries sight messages to the brain

k. tiny living parts of the body

l. to move back and forth

m. group of cells that works together

n. the colored part of the eye

o. the part of the ear that gathers sound vibrations

Name _____ Date _____

The Skeletal System

There are 206 bones in your body. They are all different sizes and shapes. Together, they make up the skeletal system. The skeletal system has several important jobs. First, it supports the body. Bones also give you shape so you will have a form. Without the bones, you would not be able to stand. The skeleton also protects the soft parts of the body, like the brain and heart. Bones also work with the muscles to help you move.

✎**Work the crossword puzzle about the skeletal system.**

Across

1. Bones and _____ work together to help you move.
3. The bones _____ the body to help you stand.
4. Bones _____ the soft body parts.

Down

2. All 206 bones make up the _____ system.
3. You have _____ and form because of bones.

How Bones Join

✎Each group of drawings and symbols gives you the clues needed to name a type of movable joint. Then answer the questions.

1. 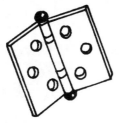 _____

2. 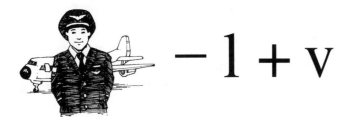 _____

3.  _____

4. Compare the function of the types of joints you listed above.

_____

_____

_____

5. Give an example of a place on your body where each kind of joint is found.

_____

_____

_____

Name _____ Date _____

Skeleton Skills

••

✎Label the skeleton with the names of the bones listed below. Use a
health book if you need to.

backbone	ribs	cranium	breastbone
jaw	femur	humerus	pelvis

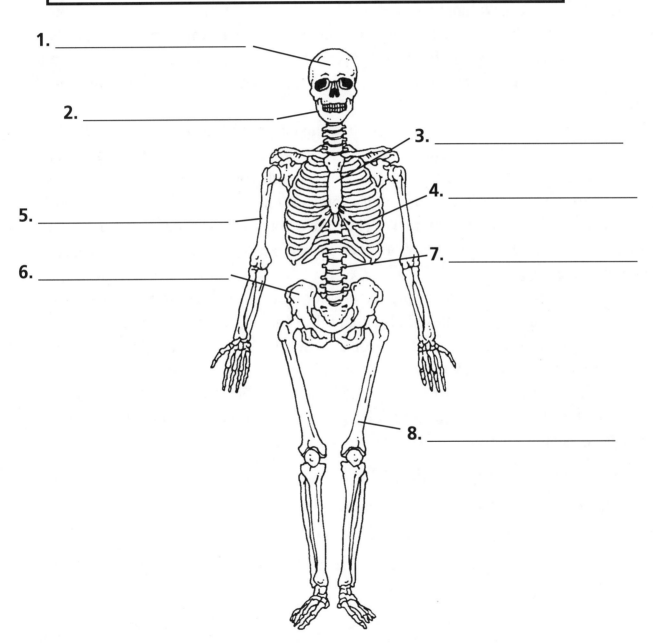

1. _____

2. _____

3. _____

4. _____

5. _____

6. _____

7. _____

8. _____

Unit 2: Systems That Shape You
Health 5, SV 2707-3

The Muscular System

The muscular system produces movement. There are over 600 different muscles in your body. Muscles cover the skeleton. They also line the walls of some organs, such as the heart and stomach. Tendons attach muscles to bones.

Muscles can be voluntary and involuntary. Voluntary muscles are the ones that you can control. You can tell them when to move. Most voluntary muscles are attached to bones. Involuntary muscles, like those of the heart, move without your having to think about them. The muscles that control your eyelids may seem like voluntary muscles. You can blink your eyes when you want to. However, you cannot keep your eyes from blinking when they need to! You do not have complete control over them.

Muscles cause movement by contracting or getting shorter and firmer. This action pulls on the bones or other body structures. Muscles move the blood through your body. They also move food and wastes through your body.

Muscle tone is achieved through exercise. If a person has good muscle tone, the muscles do not completely relax. They are always slightly contracted. For you to have good muscle tone, plenty of blood needs to reach the muscle cells. This requires exercise.

There are three types of muscles in your body. Each type of muscle cell looks different. The smooth muscles are long and thin and pointed at each end. The stomach has smooth muscle cells. Cardiac muscles make up the heart. They branch out and weave together. Skeletal muscles are long and shaped like cylinders (similar to straws). Unlike the other muscle cells, the skeletal muscles have many nuclei. The tongue and lips are skeletal muscles, as are the biceps and triceps in your arms.

✎**Match each description with the correct word.**

_____ **1.** muscles that make up the heart   **a.** tendons

_____ **2.** muscles over which you have complete control   **b.** involuntary

_____ **3.** what muscles do to cause movement   **c.** contract

_____ **4.** necessary for muscle tone   **d.** cardiac

_____ **5.** muscle cells with many nuclei   **e.** exercise

_____ **6.** attach muscles to bones   **f.** skeletal

_____ **7.** muscles that move without conscious effort   **g.** voluntary

Name _____   Date _____

Kinds of Muscles

••

✎**Complete these exercises.**

A. Each of the following is a description of a type of muscle cell.
Rewrite the description under the proper heading below.
Descriptions:
• Muscle cells that branch out and weave together. They make up the heart.
• Long, thin, and pointed cells.
• Long, cylinder-shaped cells.

1. Skeletal Muscle _____

_____

2. Cardiac Muscle _____

_____

3. Smooth Muscle _____

_____

B. Draw a diagram that shows what muscle cells from each of the following
body parts would look like. Use a health book if you need to.

4. Biceps   **5.** Heart   **6.** Stomach

Warm Up and Cool Down

Have you ever been to a football game? Do you remember seeing the players warm up? Cold, tight muscles should be warmed up and stretched little by little. This prevents muscle injuries and muscle soreness. There are two types of warm-ups. General warm-ups are for the whole body. These exercises should take between three to five minutes. They should include some stretching, some calisthenics (like jumping jacks), and some walking and jogging. There are also specific warm-ups. These exercises help the body get ready for the sport. For example, in softball, players may throw the ball back and forth.

Cool-down exercises are just as important as warm-ups. Cool-down exercises take about ten minutes. You should gradually slow down your activity. For example, cool down after jogging by walking. Stretching should also be part of the cool-down exercises. This can prevent muscle soreness.

✎**Make a list of sports or athletics that you engage in. In the other columns, make a list of warm-up and cool-down exercises you can do.**

SPORTS	WARM UP	COOL DOWN

Name _____ Date _____

Exercise and Muscles

If you exercise regularly, you can keep your muscles strong and your body healthy. Bodies that are totally fit have four important characteristics: they are strong, flexible, well-coordinated, and can endure exercise over a long period of time.

You can do these tests to see how fit you are. Wear loose clothes and gym shoes.

1. Are your arms and shoulders strong?

Flexed-Arm Hang

Using an overhand grip, hang with your chin above the bar and with your elbows flexed. Keep your legs straight and feet free of the floor.

To pass: Hold at least 3 seconds.

Pullups

Using an overhand grip, hang with your arms and legs fully extended, feet free of the floor. Pull your body up until your chin is higher than the bar, Lower your body until your arms are fully extended. Keep pullups smooth and don't kick your legs.

To pass: Do at least 1 pullup.

2. Are your abdominal muscles strong?

Do this with a partner. Lie on your back with knees flexed, feet one foot apart. With fingers laced, grasp your hands behind your head. Have a partner hold your ankles and keep your heels in contact with the floor. Sit up and touch your right elbow to the left knee. Return to the starting position. Then, sit up and touch your left elbow to the right knee.

Go on to the next page.

Exercise and Muscles, p. 2

To pass: Check the chart below.

Ages	Amount of Exercise
10	25 situps
11	26 situps
12	30 situps

3. Are you well-coordinated?

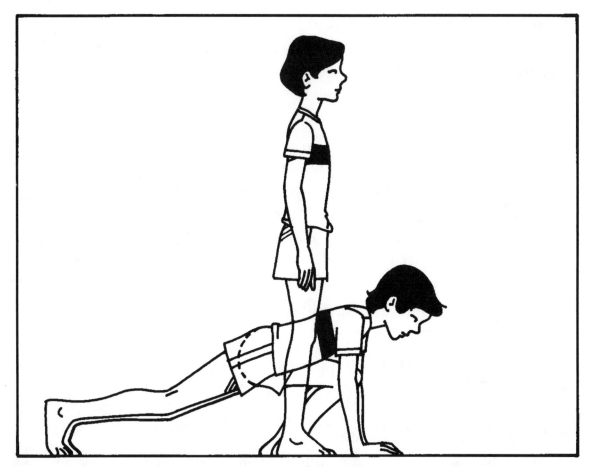

Stand straight. On count 1, bend your knees and place your hands on the floor. On count 2, thrust your legs back so your body is in a pushup position. On count 3, return to a squat position. On count 4, return to a standing position. Do as many as you can in 10 seconds.

To pass: You should do at least 4 squat thrusts in 10 seconds.

Name _____ Date _____

Muscle Tone

How strong you are depends on your muscle "tone." Good muscle tone means that your muscle cells are well-nourished. Exercising brings blood carrying food to the muscle cells. In this activity, you will measure the strength of some of your muscles. Work with a partner.

Materials:

textbook   watch with second hand   clear desktop

Do This:

1. Stretch your left arm out on the desktop so the backs of your upper arm, elbow, lower arm, and hand are all touching the desktop. Ask your partner to put the textbook in your outstretched hand. Grasp the book firmly.

2. Raise the book toward your head. Count how many times you can touch the top of your head with the textbook in 30 seconds. Record your data.

3. Rest for 1 minute. Repeat with your right arm. Then, have your partner do the activity.

Number of lifts

| **Left arm** _____ | **Right arm** _____ |

✎Answer these questions.

1. Study your data. Which of your arms had the better muscle tone?

_____

2. Make a hypothesis that explains any differences between the strength of your right and left arms.

_____

_____

3. What exercises could you do to strengthen the muscles of your arms?

_____

4. Would it be easier to improve muscle tone for voluntary muscles or involuntary muscles? Explain.

_____

Name _____ Date _____

The Circulatory System

The circulatory system and the respiratory system work together to bring oxygen and nutrients to the body cells and to remove carbon dioxide from the cells.

To follow the blood through the circulatory system, start in the heart—the right atrium, to be exact. As one valve opens, blood that needs oxygen flows from the heart. The valve closes, and another valve opens, allowing the blood to proceed to the lungs. In the lungs, the blood cells get the oxygen they need. They also get rid of carbon dioxide. As red blood cells take in oxygen and give up carbon dioxide, they change in color from dark red to bright red. The blood then leaves the lungs and passes through the heart again—this time through the left ventricle. The heart pumps it through the large arteries into the smaller arteries and capillaries throughout the body. There, oxygen and nutrients are distributed to all the other cells, and wastes are picked up. The blood becomes dark red again. Then the blood returns to the heart— the right atrium—to begin its trip once more.

The blood is carried away from the heart in blood vessels called *arteries*. The blood returns to the heart in blood vessels called *veins*. The smallest blood vessels, no wider than a hair, are called *capillaries*.

Each time the heart "beats," it pushes blood in two directions at once. Some of the blood goes to the lungs, and some of the blood goes to the rest of the body. If you have ever heard a heartbeat, you know that it makes a "puh-pum" type of sound. The "puh" sound is made when the valves of the heart close and push the blood one way, and the "pum" is the sound of different valves pushing the blood the other way. Each beat of the heart is a double pump. The heart pushes your blood through your body about once every minute.

✎**Draw a line from the description to the correct words.**

1. brings oxygen and nutrients to cells and takes away carbon dioxide

2. bring blood to the heart

3. take blood away from the heart

4. where cells take in oxygen and give up carbon dioxide

5. the smallest blood vessels

6. works with the circulatory system to deliver oxygen to cells

7. blood with little oxygen

8. blood with plenty of oxygen

a. veins

b. capillaries

c. bright red

d. circulatory system

e. dark red

f. arteries

g. respiratory system

h. lungs

Name _____ Date _____

The Flow of Blood

✎The diagram below shows the circulatory system of the human body.
Label the numbered parts of the circulatory system. Use a health book if
you need to.

A. Trace the pathway through which blood flows through the system so that it makes
a complete loop, beginning and ending at number 1. Use a colored pencil.

1. _____

2. _____

3. _____

4. _____

5. _____

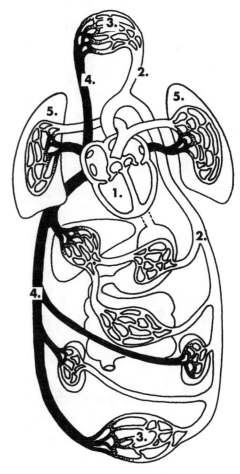

B. Match each numbered section of the
diagram with its description below.
Write the number on the line in front
of the description.

_____ **6.** smallest of all blood vessels

_____ **7.** where red blood cells drop
off carbon dioxide and
pick up oxygen

_____ **8.** carries blood away from the heart

_____ **9.** pumps blood throughout the body

_____ **10.** carries blood to the heart

Blood Cells

Red blood cells look like tiny flattened basketballs. Their red color comes from a substance in the cells called hemoglobin. Hemoglobin picks up oxygen in the lungs and carries it to all the cells of the body. Sometimes red blood cells move alone in the blood. At other times they travel in rows that look like stacks of coins. Red blood cells are made inside bones. Unlike most blood cells, a red blood cell has no nucleus. Red blood cells live about four months. Old ones are removed by the white blood cells. One milliliter of blood has between four million and six million red blood cells. If all the red blood cells from an adult's body were placed side by side, they would go around the Earth four times.

White blood cells look different from red blood cells, and they do different work. They surround and destroy invading bacteria. White blood cells are large and contain nuclei. They have irregular shapes. Some are made in the same bones as the red blood cells. Others are made in special glands. Some white blood cells live only a few days. In one milliliter of blood, there are between 5,000 and 10,000 white blood cells. When bacteria enter a person's body, the number increases.

✎**Read these statements. Underline the ones that are true.**

1. A red blood cell has a nucleus.

2. Red blood cells contain hemoglobin.

3. Red blood cells are made inside bones.

4. You have more white blood cells than red blood cells.

5. White blood cells are larger than red blood cells.

6. Red blood cells remove old white blood cells.

7. White blood cells look like flattened basketballs.

8. Some white blood cells live only a few days.

9. One milliliter of blood may have five million red blood cells.

10. When bacteria enter your body, the number of white blood cells increases.

34

Name _____ Date _____

The Digestive System

The digestive system breaks down food into nutrients. The nutrients are needed by the body for energy. As food enters your mouth, saliva mixes with the food to begin the process. From there, the food moves down the esophagus into the stomach. The stomach has juices with chemicals that break down the food even more. The food then travels to the small intestine. Its last stop is the large intestine. Then, the waste not used by the body is removed.

The parts of the digestive system are numbered on the drawing. Write the names of the parts on the lines. Then describe the digestive function of teeth, saliva, and gastric juices on the lines provided. Use a health book if you need to.

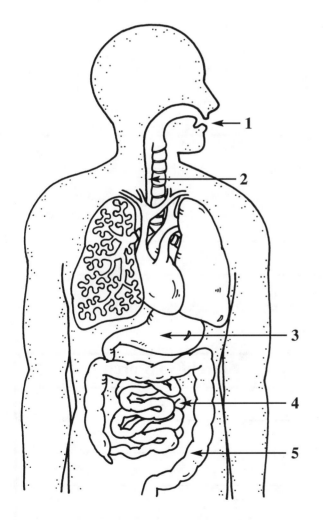

1. _____

2. _____

3. _____

4. _____

5. _____

6. teeth: _____

_____

7. saliva: _____

_____

8. gastric juices: _____

_____

Unit 3: All Systems Go!
Health 5, SV 2707-3

Name _____ Date _____

Saliva

• •

The digestion of food begins in your mouth. Your saliva contains an enzyme that breaks down starches into sugars. You can show that the digestion of starches begins in your mouth.

Materials:

plain, unsalted soda cracker
variety of foods such as bread, unsweetened cereal, peanuts, celery

✎Answer these questions.

1. A cracker contains starch. Take a bite of the cracker. How does it taste?

_____

2. Continue to chew the cracker for one minute.

How does it taste? _____

Why does it taste this way? _____

_____

_____

3. Now test some other foods. How can you find out if they contain starch?

_____

_____

4. Record your results in the chart below. Compare your results with those of your classmates.

Types of Food	Starch/No Starch
cracker	starch

The Excretory System

The excretory system removes liquid and solid wastes from the body. Liquid waste, called urine, is extra water that is filled with harmful chemicals. The kidneys are the main organs that help to remove the water from the body. Once the kidneys have removed water, salt, and other chemicals, the urine is collected in the bladder until it is emptied.

The solid waste is partly digested food that leaves the stomach and enters the small intestine. In the small intestine, the food is broken down even more and dissolved with water. Then, it diffuses through the intestine walls into the bloodstream. The remaining food is waste. It travels through the large intestine and into the rectum. Muscles in the rectum push the waste out.

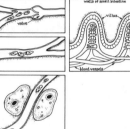

You can make a model of the wall of the small intestine to show that only dissolved substances will pass through the walls.

Materials:

paper towel	cinnamon	funnel
teaspoon	salt	two clear glasses
warm water		

Do This:

1. Pour water into one glass. Add two teaspoons of salt. Stir until the salt has dissolved.

_____

2. Add two teaspoons of cinnamon. Stir again. Does the cinnamon dissolve?

_____

3. Fold the paper towel in quarters.

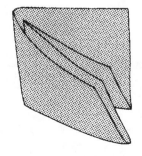

Go on to the next page.

The Excretory System, p. 2

● ●

4. Open one side of the paper towel so that it forms a filter. It will act like the wall of the small intestine.

5. Place your filter in the funnel. Place the funnel on top of the empty glass. Pour the mixture through.
What remains in the filter?_____

6. Taste the water that has been filtered.
How does it taste? _____

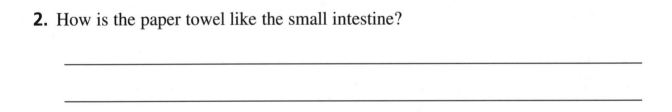

✎**Answer these questions.**

1. What passed through the filter?

_____

_____

_____

2. How is the paper towel like the small intestine?

_____

_____

_____

3. What needs to be done in the body to the cinnamon before it can pass through the walls of the small intestine?

_____

_____

_____

Name _____ Date _____

The Respiratory System

The respiratory system is responsible for the exchange of gases in the cells of the body. When you inhale, air passes through your nose, down your windpipe, and into two tubes called *bronchial tubes.* These tubes lead into your lungs. The tubes branch many times, like a tree, so that your lungs are filled with tiny tubes. The smallest tubes can only be seen with a microscope. At the ends of these tubes are air sacs.

Air is moved from the air sacs into the cells of the body by diffusion. This is the movement of a substance from an area with a lot of that substance to an area with less of that substance. When the oxygen-poor cells arrive in the lungs from the heart, the oxygen moves into the cells. The carbon dioxide, on the other hand, is more concentrated in the cells, so it moves out of the cells and into the air sacs. When you exhale, the carbon dioxide leaves your body by the same path by which the oxygen entered.

Breathing is only a partly voluntary movement. Part of the reason that you breathe is involuntary. It is caused by the movement of muscles called the *diaphragm.* This is a sheet of muscles beneath your lungs. When the diaphragm moves downward, it increases the space around the lungs, causing air to rush into your lungs. When the diaphragm moves up, it decreases the space around your lungs, and the air rushes out.

✎**Do this crossword puzzle about the respiratory system.**

Across

4. the system that brings oxygen to cells

6. the organ in which the oxygen-carbon dioxide exchange takes place

7. where oxygen goes when it leaves your nose

8. the outside organ that helps you breathe

Down

1. a sheet of muscles below your lungs

2. the tubes that lead into your lung

3. the way oxygen gets into cells

5. microscopic pocket of air in the lungs

Unit 3: All Systems Go!
Health 5, SV 2707-3

Name _____   Date _____

Respiration Rates

In and out. In and out. Without even having to think about it, you constantly breathe—while you're reading this, while you eat a snack, even while you sleep. With each breath, your body gets the oxygen it needs and gives off carbon dioxide. Find out the number of times you breathe during the day.

Materials:

stopwatch, watch, or clock with second hand
calculator

Do This:

1. Your partner will tell you when to start—and 60 seconds later will tell you when to stop.
2. Sit very still. When your partner says "go," start counting your breaths. Remember, breathing in once and then breathing out counts as one breath.
3. Write your number of breaths in the space marked *1 minute* in the table below.
4. Finish filling in the table below. To find out your number of breaths in an hour, multiply the number of breaths in *1 minute* by 60. To find out how often you breathe in a day, multiply the number of breaths in an hour by 24. Multiply that number by 365 to find the breaths in a year.

Number of Breaths			
1 minute	1 hour	1 day	1 year

✎Answer these questions.

1. Do you think your breathing rate, or how fast you breathe, can change? Explain your response.

_____

2. Test your response to the question above. Run in place for 30 seconds. Then repeat steps 1–3. Describe what happens.

_____

_____

Name _____ Date _____

Are You a Windbag?

You can find out how much air your lungs can hold.

Materials:

large clear jug   rubber tubing, about 40 cm long   tape
piece of wax paper   measuring cup   sink or large basin
pencil   water

Do This:

1. Place a strip of tape on the outside of the jug, from top to bottom.
2. Pour 100 mL of water into the jug. Then, draw a line on the tape to mark the water level. Repeat this step until the jug is full of water.
3. Fill the sink or basin about half full of water.
4. Fold the wax paper several times. Hold it tightly over the top of the jug. Being careful not to spill any water, turn the jug upside down. Set it on the bottom of the sink.
5. Guide one end of the rubber tubing into the mouth of the jug. Hold a finger over the end of the tubing.
6. Take a deep breath. Hold the breath, and put the tube in your mouth. Blow through the tube until you cannot blow anymore. When you stop to take another breath, hold your finger over the tubing.
7. Observe the water level in the jug. Ask a classmate to record this measurement for you.

Observations

1. Volume of air blown out _____ mL
   (water level in milliliters left in the jug)

2. Volume of air always in the lungs _____ mL
   (You cannot blow all the air out of your lungs.)

3. Add to find the total volume of air your lungs can hold. _____ mL

How does this activity measure the air in your lungs? As you breathe out, the air pushed the water out of the jug. The amount of water you push out is the same as the amount of air you breathe out.

Unit 3: All Systems Go!
Health 5, SV 2707-3

The Endocrine System

Look around at your classmates. Notice that they are not all the same height. There are several reasons for this. Everyone is born with a set of traits he or she received from his or her parents. If both of your parents are tall, you will probably also be tall. If both are short, you will probably be short. If one of your parents is tall and one short, you may be medium height. Another reason for the difference in your classmates' heights is that people have different growth patterns. The endocrine system controls the growth and development of the body. One person may grow faster in the beginning, yet end up shorter than someone else who started later. It may take you longer to reach the same height as one of your classmates.

This bar graph shows the growth of one student from age 1 to 10.

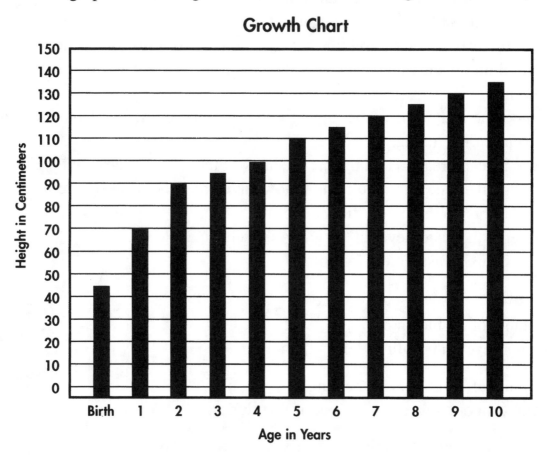

Growth Chart

A bar graph shows information about something and helps you compare numbers or amounts. Each bar in this graph represents the number of centimeters tall that the student was at a certain age. As you can see, the student grew taller each year.

Go on to the next page.

The Endocrine System, p. 2

Suppose you want to know how tall the student was at the age of 1. Find "Age in Years" at the bottom of the graph. The numbers at the bottom show age from 1 to 10 years. The numbers along the left side stand for different heights from 0 to 150 centimeters (0–59 in.). To find the student's height at 1 year, find the bar marked "1." The top of the bar is the same height as 70 cm (27 in.). So the student was 70 cm (27 in.) tall at 1 year of age.

✎**Answer these questions.**

1. How tall was the student at 2 years of age?

   _____

2. How much did the student grow between ages 1 and 2?

   _____

3. Notice the bar that stands for the student's height at 3 years. It is about halfway between 90 cm (35 in.) and 100 cm (39 in.). What was the student's height at age 3?

   _____

4. How much taller was the student at age 3 than at age 2?

   _____

5. Did the student grow more between the first and second years or between the second and third years?

   _____

6. How tall was the student at 7 years old?

   _____

7. Between what ages did the student grow exactly 10 cm?

   _____

8. During which two years did the student grow the most?

   _____

9. How many centimeters did the student grow from age 1 to 10?

   _____

The Reproductive System

All living things must reproduce, or make more living things like themselves. If a species did not reproduce, all living things of its kind would die out. The reproductive system of humans allows people to make more humans, or to have children.

When people have children, they pass on certain traits and characteristics. This is called *heredity*. Heredity affects the way you look and the way you act. You may have noticed that when adults look at a new baby, they often talk about which parent the baby looks like. This is because the baby has inherited its looks from its parents. As a child grows, there may be times when the child looks more like the mother, and times when the child looks more like the father. There will be certain things the child does that will remind people of the mother or the father, or even some other relative. All these things are inherited. Other things, such as likes and dislikes and personal fitness, are not inherited. These are the result of the person's lifestyle and environment.

When you study cells, you learn that the nucleus of a cell contains chromosomes. On the chromosomes are genes. Genes determine how offspring will look and act. Each child receives genes from both parents, but some genes are stronger than others are. These genes are called *dominant*. The weaker genes are called *recessive*.

Here is an example. The gene for brown hair is a dominant gene. We say that brown hair is a dominant trait. Blond hair is a recessive trait. If both parents have brown hair, their children will probably have brown hair. If one parent has brown hair, and the other parent has blond hair, the children will still likely have brown hair, but it is possible for a child to have blond hair. If both parents are blond, then the children will probably be blond.

The combinations can be seen in a chart like this. A brown-haired father may carry a blond-haired gene, because the brown-haired gene will dominate. He may pass on genes like this: Bb

A blond-haired mother cannot have a brown-haired gene. She must pass on genes like this: bb

To see what combinations of genes the children can receive, we can make a chart.

	B	b
b	Bb	bb
b	Bb	bb

In this family, it is possible that half of the children could have blond hair, or there is a 50% chance that a child could have blond hair.

Go on to the next page.

The Reproductive System, p. 2

If the father had not had a blond gene, he would have passed on genes like this: BB. Now what do the combinations look like? Fill in the chart. How many children can have blond hair now?

	B	B
b		
b		

There are sometimes exceptions to the rules, but they hold true most of the time.

Look at your own family. Can you tell which traits, or characteristics, you received from each of your parents? Do you have the same mannerisms as your father or your mother?

✎Make a chart about your family. You may wish to consider other close relatives as well. What family resemblances do you see?

Family Member	Hair Color	Eye Color	Height	Shape of Face	Mannerisms You Share

Name _____ Date _____

Systems Working Together

Remember:
- Cells are the basic units of all living things.
- Groups of cells with the same function are called tissues.
- Groups of tissues with the same function are called organs.
- Organs with related functions belong to a system.

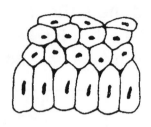

✎**Match the terms at the right with the definitions on the left.**

_____ **1.** a body structure made of different kinds of tissues that work together to do a specific job

_____ **2.** groups of cells with the same structure and function

_____ **3.** the basic unit of structure and function of an organism

_____ **4.** fluid tissue that moves from place to place

_____ **5.** a living thing that carries out all life functions

_____ **6.** a group of organs that works together to do a job

a. cell

b. tissues

c. organ

d. system

e. organism

f. blood

Systems in the body work together to get things done. The digestive system, the circulatory system, and the respiratory system work together to provide your body cells with food and oxygen they need to function. The digestive system turns the food you eat into nutrients that the body can use. At the same time, the respiratory system brings oxygen into the lungs. Oxygen passes from the lungs into the circulatory system, and nutrients pass from the small intestines into the circulatory system. In the circulatory system, the blood carries the oxygen and nutrients to all the cells of the body.

7. Can you think of another way that the systems of the body work together?

_____

_____

_____

_____

46

What Keeps You Healthy?

A habit is an activity you do so many times that it becomes automatic. Brushing your teeth every day is a good habit. Smoking cigarettes is a bad habit. All of your habits together are called your *lifestyle*. Some lifestyle habits can help you stay healthy. You need to begin good health habits when you are young. This will help you stay healthy for a long time.

Many scientists have studied lifestyles. They have discovered that seven health habits are very important. Following the habits listed below can help you stay healthy. Do you follow all these habits?

1. Never smoke cigarettes.
2. Exercise every day.
3. Use little or no alcohol.
4. Sleep seven or eight hours every night.
5. Eat breakfast every day.
6. Do not eat many snacks between meals.
7. Keep your weight right—not too thin and not too fat.

✎**Below are scrambled words about health habits. Decode the words and write them in the spaces to the right. Then, use each of the words to write a "health sentence."**

1. L L O O H A C ____ ⃝ ____ ____ ____ ____ ⃝

2. G T I W H E ____ ⃝ ____ ____ ____ ____

3. A F T ⃝ ____ ____

4. R A K E B A F S T ____ ____ ⃝ ____ ____ ____ ____ ____ ____

5. Y L E T H A H ____ ____ ____ ⃝ ____ ⃝ ____

6. P S E E L ⃝ ____ ____ ____ ____

7. X I E E E C S R ____ ____ ____ ____ ⃝ ____ ____

Now, unscramble the circled letters to form the secret word.

____ ____ ____ ____ ____ ____ ____ ____ ____ ____

Health
Grade Five
Answer Key

p. 3   1. D 2. A 3. B 4. A 5. C 6. D 7. C

p. 4   8. D 9. B 10. C 11. A 12. B 13. B 14. D

p. 5   1. organ 2. tissue 3. tissue 4. organ 5. organ 6. organism
7. system 8. system 9. tissue 10. organ 11. tissue 12. cell

p. 6   1. red blood cells 2. white blood cells 3. bone cells
4. smooth muscle cells 5. heart muscle cells
6. skeletal muscle cells 7. neurons 8. covering cells

p. 7   1. circulatory 2. muscular 3. endocrine 4. skeletal
5. integumentary 6. reproductive 7. respiratory 8. digestive
9. excretory 10. nervous

p. 8   1. smell, touch, hearing, sight, taste 2. brain 3. Possible
answer: The senses become blocked. The messages that
are sent to the brain cannot get through.

p. 10   1. The first participant should smell the perfume in ten to
twenty seconds. 2. Answers will vary. 3. Differences in the
detection times were due to the distances of the participants
from the perfume and the acuteness of the smell detectors in
their noses. Also, some participants may have allergies, colds,
or an impaired sense of smell.

p. 11   1. lens 2. pupil 3. iris 4. retina 5. optic nerve

p. 12   1. touch, temperature, pain, pressure 2. Answers may vary.
There are more nerve endings in the fingers because the
fingers help us learn about our world through touch.
3. The person would get burned.

p. 14   1. The uncut apple stayed fresh, or started to decay after
several days. The cut apple decayed quickly. The skin of the
uncut apple protected the apple from things that could harm it.
2. The skin of the apple protects it from harmful things. The
skin of a person will keep harmful things, like disease, from
entering the body, too.

p. 15   1. The answers are in the following order: 2, 5, 1, 4, 6, 3.

p. 16   1.A. Sound vibrations caused by the instruments reach the
eardrum. The vibrating eardrum passes the message to
nearby bones. Bones vibrate and pass the message to the
auditory nerve. Auditory nerves carry the message to the
brain. B. 1. Answers will vary. 2. Louder: More sound
vibrations would be caught and sent to the eardrum.

p. 17   1. jackhammer, gunshots at firing range, explosions
2. (talking) 25 decibels – (whispering) 10 decibels = 15
decibels 3. about 50 decibels

p. 18   1. taste buds 2. taste nerves 3. brain 4. bitter

p. 20   1. Answers will vary. 2. Answers will vary. 3. By holding the
nose closed, the taster's sense of smell was not involved in the
identification process. The sense of taste is affected by the
sense of smell. 4. The results would probably be different if
the tasters had been able to see the food. After seeing the
food, the tasters would probably decide what it tasted like
before actually tasting the food sample. 5. It is likely that the
results would be different if the tasters did not hold their noses
since odor information would reach the brain.

p. 21   1. Answers will vary. 2. Your eye signaled your brain, which
told your body when to react.

p. 22   1. l 2. h 3. i 4. k 5. a 6. e 7. n 8. d 9. j 10. c 11. g 12. m
13. f 14. o 15. b

p. 23   Across: 1. muscles 3. support 4. protect Down: 2. skeletal
3. shape

p. 24   1. hinge 2. ball and socket 3. pivot 4. The hinge joint allows
bones to move back and forth or up and down. The ball and
socket joint allows bones to move in any direction. The pivot
joint allows bones to move around and back. 5. The elbow is
a hinge joint. The shoulder has a ball and socket joint. The
skull and backbone form a pivot joint.

p. 25   1. cranium 2. jaw 3. breastbone 4. ribs 5. humerus
6. pelvis 7. backbone 8. femur

p. 26   1. d 2. g 3. c 4. e 5. f 6. a 7. b

p. 27   A. 1. Long, cylinder-shaped cells 2. Muscle cells that branch
out and weave together. They make up the heart. 3. Long,
thin and pointed cells. B. 4.–6. Check students' drawings.

p. 31   1. Answers will vary. 2. One arm is used more than the other.
The more exercise the muscles get, the better the muscle
tone. 3. pushups, weight lifting, etc. 4. It would be easier to
improve the tone of your voluntary muscles because you can
exercise them.

p. 32   1. d 2. a 3. f 4. h 5. b 6. g 7. e 8. c

p. 33   A. 1. heart 2. artery 3. capillaries 4. vein 5. lungs B. 6. 3
7. 5 8. 2 9. 1 10. 4

p. 34   1. Students underline statements 2, 3, 5, 8, 9, 10.

p. 35   1. mouth 2. esophagus 3. stomach 4. small intestine
5. large intestine 6. Teeth chew food. 7. Saliva softens food.
8. Gastric juices change food into a liquid.

p. 36   1. Answers will vary. 2. It should taste sweet. An enzyme in
saliva has changed some of the starch to sugar. 3. Chew
them. If they contain starch, they will taste sweet after a bit.

p. 37   2. no

p. 38   5. cinnamon 6. salty 1. salt and water 2. The paper towel
filtered foods that were not broken down. The small intestine
does the same thing. It filters food too large to pass through to
the bloodstream. 3. It must be digested.

p. 39   Across: 4. respiratory 6. lungs 7. windpipe 8. nose
Down: 1. diaphragm 2. bronchial 3. diffusion 5. sac

p. 40   1. Responses will vary, but may include the fact that
respiration rate increases with activity. 2. The respiration
rate increases.

p. 41   1.–3. Answers will vary.

p. 43   1. 90 cm (35 in.) 2. 20 cm (9 in.) 3. about 95 cm (about 38
in.) 4. about 5 cm (about 2 in.) 5. The student grew more
between the first and second years of age. 6. 120 cm (47 in.)
7. The student grew 10 cm (4 in.) between 4 and 5 years of
age. 8. The student grew the most between the first and
second years of age. 9. The student grew from 70 cm (27 in.)
to 135 cm (53 in.).

p. 45   1. Chart: Bb, Bb, Bb, Bb; None of the children are likely to
have blond hair.

p. 46   1. c 2. b 3. a 4. f 5. e 6. d 7. Answers will vary.
Check students' responses.

p. 47   1. alcohol 2. weight 3. fat 4. breakfast 5. healthy
6. sleep 7. exercise Secret Word: lifestyle

Answer Key
Health 5, SV 2707-3